THE TUDORS

FIONA REYNOLDSON

WAYLAND

HISTORY STARTS HERE!
The Tudors
OTHER TITLES IN THE SERIES
The Ancient Egyptians • The Ancient Greeks
• The Ancient Romans

Produced for Wayland Publishers Limited by
Roger Coote Publishing
Gissing's Farm
Fressingfield
Suffolk IP21 5SH
England

Designer: Victoria Webb
Cover design: Paul Cherill
Editor: Alex Edmonds
Illustrations: Michael Posen

© Wayland 1999

First published in Great Britain in 1999 by Wayland Publishers Ltd

Reprinted in 2000 by Wayland,
A division of Hachette Children's Books

Paperback edition published in 2003 by Wayland
This edition published in 2008 by Wayland

Reprinted in 2008 and 2009 by Wayland

Wayland
338 Euston Road
London NW1 3BH

British Library Cataloguing in Publication Data
Reynoldson, Fiona
The Tudors. – (History starts here)
  1. Great Britain – History – Tudors, 1485-1603
  – Juvenile literature
  I. Title
  942'.05

ISBN: 978-0-7502-5394-9

Printed and bound in China

Front cover picture: Queen Elizabeth I.
Title page picture: King Henry VIII and his jester, Will Summers.
Picture Acknowledgements:
AKG London Ltd: 4; The Bridgeman Art Library: 10, 14, 15; CM Dixon: 8, 12, 20;
Mary Evans Picture Library: 17, 18-19, 19, 22, 25, 27; ET Archive: front cover, 1,
7, 9, 11, 21, 28, 29.
Every attempt has been made to clear copyright for this edition. Should there be any inadvertent
omission please apply to the publisher for rectification.

Wayland is a division of Hachette Children's Books, an Hachette UK company
www.hachette.co.uk

CONTENTS

During Tudor times, England became a very powerful country. The very first Tudor king was Henry VII, who became king when he won the Battle of Bosworth Field in 1485.

When Henry VII died, his son Henry VIII became king. Then, when Henry died, his son Edward VI became king. And he was followed by his sisters Mary and Elizabeth.

Elizabeth was the last of the Tudors and she died in 1603. She was known as Elizabeth I. By the end of Elizabeth's reign England was a very peaceful country.

Henry VII was one of the first English rulers to encourage explorers to travel all round the world. In this picture he is standing next to a map of part of North America. There are several explorers standing behind him.

Queen Elizabeth I was Henry VII's grand-daughter. She was a very popular ruler.

TOWNS

In Tudor times the population grew a lot. More and more people moved from the countryside to the towns. They went to look for work. London and other towns grew bigger because of this.

The streets of London were crowded and dirty. The houses were often poorly built and unsafe.

This large town house was probably built for a wealthy Tudor merchant.

Carts, carrying goods to and from the markets, filled the narrow streets of the towns. Street sellers shouted out the prices of their goods. Farmers from the country drove animals through the streets to market. The towns were noisy, crowded and dirty. Because the towns were so dirty, it was difficult to stop diseases from spreading. Many poor people became very ill and died.

THE COUNTRYSIDE

The woodcutter and shepherd in this picture are dressed in loose clothes so they can work comfortably.

Most people still lived in the countryside in Tudor times. They lived on farms and in villages. Farmers kept animals such as cows, sheep and pigs and they grew wheat, barley and other crops. They lived on the food they grew. If they had any left over, they took it to market in the nearest town to sell.

Going to market was a chance to meet friends, make some money and buy items such as candles, shoes and ribbons.

Most country people worked from dawn to dusk on farms. They got up early and fed the animals. Then they went to work in the fields. At night they sat round the fire and ate plain food, such as thick soup that had cooked all day over the fire. Life was very hard in the countryside.

All the guests at this wedding party are dressed in their best clothes. The party is being held at the home of a wealthy farmer.

THE RICH

Rich people loved to wear the latest fashions. They also loved big, beautiful houses with expensive things in. They had glass in the windows, which was a luxury, and plenty of different rooms to live in.

These rich people are dressed in silk and velvet. The children are dressed in the same style of clothes as the adults.

LORDS AND MERCHANTS

Some rich people were Lords and helped the king or queen to run the country. Other rich people were merchants. They bought and sold goods such as wines, silks, fish and wool.

Rich people lived in big houses with many rooms. Often the rooms were very large. This made them difficult to keep warm.

Rich people often owned a lot of land. They hunted on the land for wild animals, such as deer and wild boar, which they caught and had cooked. The rich had lots of servants to cook, clean and run the house. Their servants would also farm the land for them.

THE POOR

Poor people owned very little. They lived in one-room cottages made of mud and sticks. There was no glass in their windows and their houses were cold and draughty. Most days were spent getting enough food to eat and some sticks to burn on the fire. When there was not enough food, or the weather was bad, poor people often died from cold and hunger.

Poor people had to work nearly every day. Often they only earned enough money to buy food and clothing.

Poor people lived in one-room cottages. The fire was their only way of keeping warm. They sat round the fire to eat.

Sometimes poor people did not even have a home to live in. They slept under hedges and in church porches. They wore rags and went barefoot. Often they had to beg to get food.

13

CHILDREN

Most children from rich families went to school and learnt how to read and write. Poor families tried to send their children to school too, but usually only the boys would go. Girls would stay at home and learn how to cook and clean.

Poor boys and girls from the country often lived so far from their school that their parents made them stay at home and work on the farmland.

Young girls from rich families were taught how to run a big house and manage servants. Boys learnt how to run a business or a farm.

Rich children wore clothes made of silk, velvet and other expensive fabrics.

Rich Tudor children played with dolls, toy soldiers and drums. When they were outside they would play with hoops and balls. Poor children had to play with home-made toys.

Ordinary people needed cheap, hard-wearing, warm clothes. They usually wore clothes made of wool. Men wore trousers to the knee, long woollen socks and leather boots. Often, working men wore sleeveless leather jackets.

Rich people wore clothes made of silk and velvet. In winter their clothes were trimmed with fur. Women wore long dresses. Their skirts were held in shape with a hoop of wood called a farthingale.

Poor people could not afford many clothes. To make them last longer, they patched them when they wore out.

THE CLOTHES OF THE RICH

Rich people loved to show off their riches. They wore bright colours and jewels in their hats. They even had jewels sewn on their clothes.

Rich men wore
padded jackets,
short padded
trousers and long
socks or stockings.

FOOD

Most ordinary people lived on bread and soup, which was made from home-grown vegetables and oatmeal. Sometimes there might be some meat in the soup.

Storing food was hard without fridges. People tried to keep foods, such as meat or fish, for longer by rubbing salt into them.

Cooks used fresh vegetables and meat in the summer. In winter they used salted meat and dried or pickled vegetables.

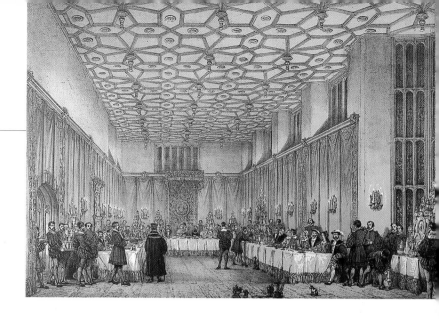

Very rich people, such as the king, ate lots of meat all the time. There were often big feasts. Then deer, pheasants and wild boar were roasted whole in the huge kitchens. There were baked fish from the rivers and lakes, and rich puddings of fruit and marzipan.

Henry VIII held huge feasts in his palace at Hampton Court.

RELIGION

The Church played a large part in the lives of the Tudor people. At the beginning of Tudor times, almost everyone in England was a Roman Catholic. The head of the Roman Catholic Church was the Pope. However, many people did not want the Pope to be leader of the Church. They were called Protestants.

When the Tudor king Henry VIII wanted to divorce his first wife, the Pope would not let him. So Henry made himself Head of the Church in England.

This picture shows the ruins of Fountains Abbey. When Henry VIII took control of the Church of England, his soldiers destroyed and stole riches from many English monasteries like this one.

Henry VIII married six times to find a wife who could give him a son. His third wife, Jane Seymour, died giving birth to his only son, Edward.

HAVING FUN

Rich and poor people liked to enjoy themselves. Tudor people enjoyed rough sports. They loved to watch dogs fighting with bulls and bears, or they went to watch cockerels fighting to the death. Young men played football, which was then known as a very rough game.

Tudor people loved hunting. Rich people hunted boar and deer for sport. The poor hunted rabbits and other animals for food.

The Tudors enjoyed going to the theatre. Many open-air theatres were built in Tudor times.

The English were also known for their love of music and the theatre. People gathered together in the evening to sing and dance or to play musical instruments. Some people went to the theatre to see new plays by the most famous English playwright of all, William Shakespeare.

WAR AND SHIPS

During Tudor times, Spain and England went to war. King Philip of Spain sent a great fleet of ships, full of soldiers and sailors, to invade England. Queen Elizabeth I and her court had spent a lot of money on building lighter, faster ships for the English navy. The English navy was stronger than it had ever been.

In 1588 the Spanish Armada sailed to attack England. There were twice as many Spanish ships as English ships. But the English ships were easier to sail and had better guns.

Queen Elizabeth ordered her ships to attack the Spanish. There was a great battle in the English Channel. Then a terrible storm scattered the ships and the Spanish fled for home. The English victory made Elizabeth very popular, and England became famous for its good sailors.

Elizabeth I knighted Sir Francis Drake in 1581. Four years later, he led the English ships against the Spanish Armada.

EXPLORATION

Elizabeth I encouraged people to go exploring; to look for new lands. The explorers brought tobacco and potatoes from North America and spices and silks from Asia. The English traded with the people they met and many merchants and traders became wealthy from this.

DRAKE AND RALEIGH

During Queen Elizabeth's reign Francis Drake sailed round the world. Sir Walter Raleigh went to start a settlement in Virginia in America. After this, many people went to live in America.

This map shows the routes of the great European explorers of Tudor times.

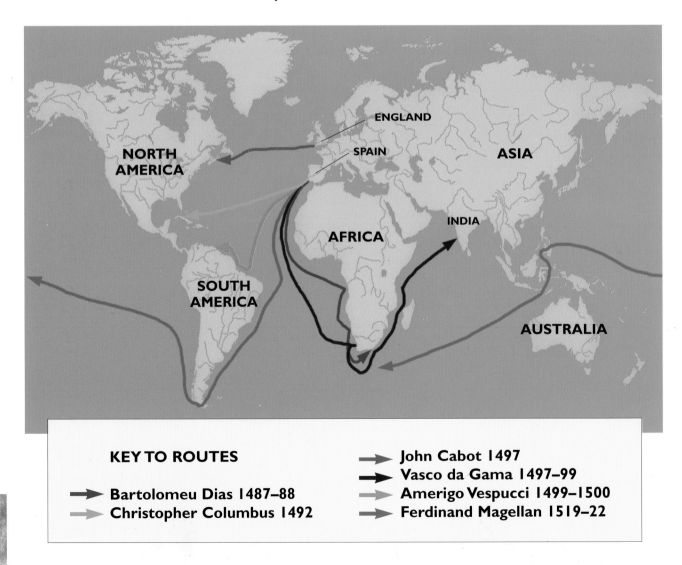

KEY TO ROUTES

→ Bartolomeu Dias 1487–88
→ Christopher Columbus 1492
→ John Cabot 1497
→ Vasco da Gama 1497–99
→ Amerigo Vespucci 1499–1500
→ Ferdinand Magellan 1519–22

When explorers, like Sir Walter Raleigh, came across a new country they were shocked by how different the people were to themselves. They spoke different languages, wore different clothes and lived very differently to the Tudor explorers.

During Tudor times, England became very powerful. It was also famous for its writers, poets and explorers. For many people in Tudor times, the trade with new lands made them richer.

However, many people were still very poor. The monasteries had been closed down by Henry VIII and were no longer there to help poor people. In Elizabeth's reign, laws were passed for the first time to help the poor and to find them work.

Many rich Tudor people built very big houses. Many of these can still be seen today. The house below is called Longleat and is in Wiltshire.

Elizabeth I had no children. When she died, in 1603, her cousin James Stuart became king of England.

Queen Elizabeth I did not marry. So when she died, she had no heirs and the throne passed on from the Tudors to the Stuart dynasty.

IMPORTANT DATES

1485 Henry VII beat Richard III at the Battle of Bosworth to become the first Tudor king.

1488 Dias sailed round the Cape of Good Hope.

1492 Christopher Columbus sailed to San Salvador, the present-day Bahamas, and proved that the world was round.

1498 Vasco da Gama became the first European to find a sea route round the Cape of Good Hope to India. Henry VII gave John Cabot a boat to sail to northern China.

1509 Henry VII died. Henry VIII married Catherine of Aragon.

1527 Henry VIII asked the Pope to allow him to divorce Catherine of Aragon.

1529 Henry VIII sacked Cardinal Wolsey, the Lord Chancellor who had not persuaded the Pope to allow Henry to divorce Catherine of Aragon.

1532 Henry VIII married Anne Boleyn in secret. Henry VIII was barred from the Church by the Pope.

1534 Henry VIII was made the supreme head of the Church of England.

1536 Henry VIII had Anne Boleyn's head cut off.

1539 By this time Henry VIII had got rid of the monasteries and taken their lands.

1540 Henry VIII divorced his fourth wife, Ann of Cleves, after being married for only six months. Henry VIII married his fifth wife, Catherine Howard.

1542 Catherine Howard was executed.

1543 Henry VIII married Catherine Parr.

1546 Henry VIII died.

1547 Edward VI became king.

1553 Edward VI died. Lady Jane Grey became queen of England for nine days. Mary I became queen of England.

1554 Lady Jane Grey was beheaded at Mary I's request. Mary I married King Philip of Spain. All the religious laws passed under Henry VIII were changed.

1558 Mary I died. Elizabeth I became queen of England.

1559 Elizabeth I took power from the Pope and made the Church of England powerful again. She spent a lot of money to build up the English navy.

1580 Francis Drake returned from his voyage around the world.

1588 The English defeated the Spanish Armada.

1598 The first important law to help poor people was made. Shakespeare's play, *Twelfth Night*, opened in London.

1603 Queen Elizabeth I died.

GLOSSARY

Boar These wild pigs used to be found all over Britain.

Doublet A close-fitting woollen or leather jacket, with or without sleeves, that Tudor men wore.

Farthingdale A round frame that was used to hold a woman's skirt in shape.

Luxury Something only rich people could afford to buy.

Market A place for buying and selling goods.

Marzipan A sweet made of sugar and almonds that is used in cakes and desserts.

Merchant A person who makes a living buying and selling things.

Pheasant This large, long-tailed bird was often roasted and served at Tudor feasts.

Pope The head of the Roman Catholic Church is called the Pope.

Population The number of people living in a place.

Spanish Armada The fleet of Spanish ships that sailed to invade England in 1588.

Spices Plants and seeds that are used to flavour food.

FURTHER INFORMATION

BOOKS TO READ

History from Buildings: Tudor Britain by Stewart Ross (Watts, 2006)

Building History: Tudor Theatre by Gillian Clements (Watts, 2004)

A Tudor School by Peter Chrisp (Heinemann, 2002)

An Illustrated World of the Tudors by Peter Chrisp (Wayland, 2001)

The Facts About the Tudors and Stuarts by Dereen Taylor (Wayland, 2007)

British Heritage: The Tudors by Robert Hull (Wayland, 2007)

Reconstructed: The Tudors by Liz Gogerly (Wayland, 2005)

INDEX